D0632411

WHAT IF...?

**Other Youth Specialties books
by Les Christie**

Have You Ever...? 450 intriguing questions
guaranteed to get teenagers talking

Unfinished Sentences: 450 tantalizing
statement-starters to get teenagers
talking & thinking

Check us out at *www.YouthSpecialties.com*!

WHAT IF...?

450 Thought-Provoking Questions to
Get Teenagers Talking, Laughing,
and Thinking

Les Christie

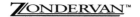

Youth Specialties

ZONDERVAN™

GRAND RAPIDS, MICHIGAN 49530 USA

What If ...? 450 Thought-Provoking Questions to Get Teenagers Talking, Laughing, and Thinking

Copyright © 1996 by Youth Specialties

Youth Specialties Books, 300 S. Pierce St., El Cajon, CA 92020, are published by Zondervan Publishing House, 5300 Patterson, S.E., Grand Rapids, MI 49530.

ISBN 0-310-20776-2

Edited by Noel Becchetti
Cover design by Proxy
Interior design by Youth Specialties

Printed in the United States of America

02 03 04 05 06 / CH / 13 12 11 10 9

Contents

To Brent and David for not only answering questions but for questioning answers.

Many, through their comments, ideas, suggestions, and encouragement, have helped bring this book to its final form. I particularly want to thank the following imaginative youth ministry students at San Jose Christian College for their invaluable assistance during some enjoyable brainstorming times: Laurel Hall, Bryan Allen, Gordon Zagar, Robin Dismore, and Amy Roberson.

For his skillful editorial direction, as well as his many recommendations, I wish to thank Noel Becchetti.

I especially want to thank Joani Schultz for allowing me to use 10 of her thoughts from the *Talk Starter* book and her buoyant spirit and continued optimism about life. Thanks also for the perceptive insights of Brewster McCloud and Russ Cantu.

The History of *What If ...?*

The questions in *What If...?* will cause you to take a deeper look at who you are and what you believe. Some of the questions are just plain fun, some even a little silly. Others are extremely serious and bring you face to face with issues many students and adults are facing.

Have fun with these questions. Change them, play with them, and add details to them. Use these questions as a point of departure and let your imagination go. The only thing I ask is that you do not answer any of the questions with a simple yes or no. Try to search out what you are thinking and feeling.

Some of the questions are designed to stretch you and some to make you feel uncomfortable. Some of the questions offer difficult choices. You will look at your past and project yourself into hypothetical situations. Don't be afraid of them. Think, use your creativity, dream. This will be quite an adventure.

This book will be helpful on those long trips in a car or bus when you want to break the tension and get the conversation going. You may want to start with some of the lighter questions and just stay with them for the trip out and look at some others for the return trip. You may want to code your favorite questions. For example, put an **F** next to the questions you think are funny and know will get a laugh. Write a **DD** next to the questions that you know will cause the group to dig deeper in the conversation. Put an **HT** next to the ones that are hot topics that will create some heated debate.

Be wise when deciding which questions to ask. If I have a student whose parents just went through a messy divorce, I wouldn't ask #36 (you found one of your parents in an affair). Be extremely sensitive with questions having to do with appearance; carefully assess certain questions' potential impact on certain students.

I recommend you discuss the questions with a trusted companion or a small group of friends with whom you feel comfortable expressing your thoughts and feelings. Begin to wrestle verbally with each other over how you reached your conclusions to the questions. It is surprising how often someone we think we know will respond to a question in a way that we would never have predicted. Part of the enjoyment of the questions is discovering the journeys people are taking in coming up with the answers they are giving. Talk about the process you went through in coming up with your responses.

You can also take this book with you for a solo journey. Get away for an hour or a day or a weekend by yourself. Find a comfortable place where you will not be disturbed and dive into the questions. One of the benefits of this book is that it allows you to gain insights without actually living through the predicaments described in the questions. You may want to record some of your thoughts to look at later or to share with a friend. I hope this book raises questions you have wanted to raise for long time but just did not know how to bring up. I hope you have an exceptional time.

How to use *What If...?*

As you approach each question, consider at least three possible follow-up questions:

What could you do?

Let your mind wander and explore all the possibilities. There are no wrong answers, so let your imagination run wild. Brainstorm, thinking of every possible way to approach the situation. Don't evaluate your answers at this point. Your task is to dream big and be creative. Have fun with all the options in front of you.

What would you do?

What do you think you would do and why would you select this course of action out of all the possibilities? What if you were in a different mood, place, or time? Would you still come to the same conclusion? Why or why not? What if you were with different people? How might they affect your decision?

What should you do?

Does the Bible have anything to say to this question? What would Jesus do if he were faced with the same set of circumstances? Why? What would your parents do? Why? What would your minister, youth minister, youth sponsors, or teachers do? Why? What would Billy Graham or Mother Teresa do? Why? You get the idea.

What If ...

1

...you found out you were adopted?

2

...you inherited a million dollars?

3

...you could be invisible?

4

...you could visit any planet?

5

...you had a week to live?

6

...you found a cure for cancer?

7

...you lost the use of your legs?

8

...you were about to throw up, sitting next to your first date on a fast amusement park ride?

9

...you knew the world would end in a month?

10

...you had superhero powers?

11

...you had to choose only five books you could read?

12

...you gained 50 pounds?

13

...you could speak to the President
for 15 minutes?

14

...you could live anywhere in the world?

15

...you could travel back in time?

16

...you found out you had AIDS?

17

...you could eat anything and not get fat?

18

...you suddenly were 70 years old?

19

...you had to relive your worst night-mare?

20

...you could breathe under water?

21

...you could be any model of automobile?

22

...you were a sports superstar?

23

...you were granted three wishes?

24

...you saw a U.F.O.?

25

...you had to rappel down a cliff?

26

...you were struck dumb?

27

...you found yourself at the
crucifixion of Jesus?

28

...your television stopped working?

29

...you could be your parents for a day?

30

...you had no parents?

31

...your head were made of clay?

32

...your touch could heal?

33

...you could show people your dreams?

34

...you could fly?

35

...you developed a vaccine that could cure all diseases?

36

...you found one of your parents in an affair?

37

...you could change the shape of your body instantly?

38

...you could be any person from the Bible's Old Testament?

39

...you could influence people's minds?

40

...you had unlimited resources to protect your home?

41

...you forgot to reserve a tuxedo or buy a formal dress for the senior prom?

42

...you didn't need to sleep?

43

...you could defy gravity?

44

...there were no laws?

45

...food had no smell?

46

...everybody looked identical?

47

...you were the tallest person alive?

48

...you accidentally killed your younger
sister's favorite pet?

49

...you could remember everything
you read, heard, or saw?

50

...you had one key that fit every lock?

51

...you could control the weather?

52

...you knew that you had one hour to
live?

53

...the sun never went down?

54

...the sun never came up?

55

...you knew the day and hour of
Christ's second coming?

56

...you were the star of a nightly TV show?

57

...no one had a conscience?

58

...you could read people's minds?

59

...your parents brought home
a homeless person?

60

...you wanted to marry someone
of another race?

61

...you could be a part of any TV family?

62

...you could ask God three questions?

63

...you could relive your happiest memory?

64

...you could always drive 30 miles over
the speed limit and not get caught?

65

...you could make it be any day of the week?

66

...you could talk to your family about anything?

67

...your pastor asked you how you liked his/her sermon?

68

...you spilled a soft drink on your pants at a party?

69

...you could relive your favorite
family tradition?

70

...you could change sexes?

71

...you could tell people when and
how they were going to die?

72

...you could be any age?

73

...you could set your own curfew time?

74

...you could never feel physical pain?

75

...your friend got a bad haircut?

76

...you could recapture one great quality
you had as a small child?

77

...you didn't have to work for a living?

78

...you had a love potion that would cause anyone who drank it to fall in love with you?

79

...someone offered you $100,000 for one of your eyes?

80

...you knew more than your parents?

81

...you had to relive your angriest
moment?

82

...you could search anyone's locker at
school?

83

...you could spend 24 hours
with anyone in the world?

84

...you could purchase a video of your
friends telling exactly what they think of
you?

85

...you could relive any family vacation?

86

...you went to a party and didn't know anyone?

87

...you could end all wars by killing one innocent person?

88

...you could make it be any holiday of the year?

89

...someone offered you $10,000 in exchange for living by yourself in a room with no windows?

90

...you could be with an old childhood friend?

91

...you could relive one day of your life?

92

...you could have a foreign exchange student from any country live with you?

93

...you were offered $5,000 to break up with your boyfriend/girlfriend?

94

...you could remove any family photo-graph from your home?

95

...you could spend a year studying any subject?

96

...God didn't exist?

97

...you found out your parents had been looking through your dresser drawers?

98

...you found out the star player of your basketball team was using drugs?

99

...you could be any cartoon character?

100

...your best friend raped your sister while they were on a date?

101

...you got $4 more change then you should have at a market?

102

...you were a nurse and botched up a surgery?

103

...you could be any animal?

104

...you had a pocket-sized device that would beep every time someone (including you) told a lie?

105

...your home were on fire and you could save only three personal items?

106

...you could wipe out any one kind of music?

107

...you were invited to go bungee jumping?

108

...you could relive any birthday?

109

...aliens offered you a ride in their space-ship?

110

...a good friend had bad breath?

111

...you could exchange bodies with anyone?

112

...you could change one thing about your family?

113

...you had a chance to sing the National Anthem at the Super Bowl?

114

...you found out your best friend has AIDS?

115

...your friends knew everything about you?

116

...you could change your name?

117

...you could choose anyone, alive or dead, to go to for advice?

118

...someone offered you $5,000 to wear your parents' clothes for a month?

119

...you could be any person from the Bible's New Testament?

120

...you could take back something you've said?

121

...you could go on worldwide television and warn people about three things?

122

...a tabletop fortune-telling machine accurately answered all your yes and no questions?

123

...you could change one thing in the Bible?

124

...you could change the legal drinking age?

125

...you could choose any dead relative
to talk with?

126

...you saw a family member committing
a serious crime?

127

...you were God?

128

...you had to give up one of your five
senses?

129

...you could find out the truth of any one trial in history?

130

...you could eliminate pain in one person?

131

...you found out your neighbors belonged to a terrorist group?

132

...you were bald?

133

...you could be any household appliance?

134

...your neighbor allowed his or her dog to regularly "fertilize" your lawn?

135

...you saw a cook sneeze in a bowl of soup delivered to the table next to you?

136

...you could keep only one of your five senses?

137

...you had one week to do anything you wanted, all expenses paid?

138

...you could ask your parents anything?

139

...you could have any occupation?

140

...you could put anything on your tombstone?

141

...you could speak any language?

142

...you got to be Santa Claus for a night?

143

...you could see any television program,
past or present?

144

...you could talk to any of your teachers,
past or present?

145

...you could speak to any public figure, past or present?

146

...you could make it be any time of the day?

147

...you could pass one thing on to the next generation?

148

...you could put five things into a time capsule to be opened in one hundred years?

149

...you could ask your grandparents anything?

150

...you went blind?

151

...your school put security cameras in the restrooms?

152

...you could have any hairstyle?

153

...you could have any hair color?

154

...you could be Plastic Man or have his powers?

155

...you had 30 seconds on live worldwide TV?

156

...you won a ride in the space shuttle?

157

...you were trapped in an earthquake-damaged building?

158

...your house burned down?

159

...you owned a radio station?

160

...you could compete on any television game show?

161

...you were given the car of your dreams?

162

...you could walk through walls?

163

...Jesus returned to earth tomorrow?

164

...you were color blind?

165

...you were buried alive?

166

...you had an extraordinary stopwatch
that could freeze everything and
everyone in the world (except you)
when you pushed the button?

167

...everything you asked for came true?

168

...you had never been born?

169

...you never married?

170

...there were no such thing as money?

171

...you got married?

172

...there were no devil?

173

...God did not love us?

174

...everybody decided not to work?

175

...you could go through a door-shaped hole
into another dimension?

176

...you lived in a Third World country?

177

...World War III were declared?

178

...people were nice?

179

...the United States had lost World War II?

180

...you could smash one and only one
thing?

181

...an atomic bomb were to fall
in 30 minutes?

182

...you had to describe your life in
three minutes?

183

...you had to describe a sunset in one
word?

184

...you had to describe loneliness in one
word?

185

...you had to face your greatest fear?

186

...you had to use another word for God?

187

...you were shipwrecked on a deserted island and could take only five things off of the sinking ship?

188

...you were asked to paint a picture?

189

...you could go into suspended animation and wake up 100 years later?

190

...you were asked to write a novel?

191

...you had to share the nicest thing that ever happened to you?

192

...you had to share the meanest thing that ever happened to you?

193

...you could alter one event in history?

194

...you could have one superhuman power?

195

...you could get rid of one personal pet peeve?

196

...you could eliminate your greatest fear?

197

...you could protest against only one
issue?

198

...you were on a deserted island and could
only have three books?

199

...you could marry anyone?

200

...you could take a stand for only one
issue?

201

...you were asked to share your proudest accomplishment?

202

...you had to define success?

203

...you had to define failure?

204

...you stuck your neck out?

205

...you had to relive your most
embarrassing moment?

206

...you swam against the current?

207

...you swam with the current?

208

...you forgave and forgot?

209

...you made up your mind to be happy?

210

...you could invent, design, or
create one thing?

211

...you stopped waiting
for your ship to come in
but instead swam out to meet it?

212

...you stopped blaming others and took
responsibility for your life?

213

...you surprised a loved one with an unexpected gift?

214

...you threw up in class?

215

...you did nice things for people who would never find out?

216

...you lost your sense of humor?

217

...you had a magic carpet?

218

...your parents told you they are
considering a divorce?

219

...you had six toes on one foot?

220

...you bent over in a school play and
split your pants?

221

...you relaxed and loosened up?

222

...you could spend an entire day riding
one amusement park ride?

223

...you kept it simple?

224

...you took time to smell the roses?

225

...you practiced empathy?

226

...you didn't expect life to be fair?

227

...you rekindled an old friendship?

228

...you were bold and courageous?

229

...you got organized?

230

...you had to relive your saddest moment?

231

...you knew when to keep silent and
when to speak up?

232

...you didn't feel sorry for yourself?

233

...you could only keep three of your photographs?

234

...the employees were on strike at your favorite store?

235

...you could watch only international, national, state, or local news?

236

...you found out someone doing the same job as you is paid $3 more an hour?

237

...a casual friend asked how much money you made?

238

...you could pick only one other student to work on a school project with you?

239

...you were a high school teacher?

240

...you broke a valuable dish at a friend's house during a party but no one knew you did it?

241

...you were a psychiatrist and a patient
admitted a felony to you?

242

...you knew someone was looking to
you as a role model?

243

...you had an expensive bicycle that
you had outgrown?

244

...you were selling a car that you knew
had something wrong with it?

245

...you were offered $100,000 to endorse a product you thought was worthless?

246

...a drunk driver killed your parents, but was acquitted on a technicality?

247

...you were 14 and a movie theater let you in for child's price because they thought you were 12?

248

...you could tell a secret to only one friend?

249

...you were ruler of the world?

250

...everyone forgot your birthday?

251

...you were one of 10 people in a lifeboat that could hold only eight?

252

...you found out you have an identical twin living in another state?

253

...you could delete one rule in your home?

254

...you could delete one rule at your school?

255

...you could pick any nickname for yourself?

256

...you could trade places with one of your classmates for a month?

257

...you never felt guilt?

258

...someone bigger than you continually
bothered you?

259

...you could do anything you
wanted for one day?

260

...on a first date, your date sees you
pick your nose?

261

...you think you should take an action because "it's the right thing to do," yet everyone is warning you not to do it?

262

...you could be any religious leader living today?

263

...you could see into the future but not be able to alter it?

264

...you knew you were going to die tonight and could communicate with only one person before you died?

265

...you could enjoy one month of incredible joy but afterwards remember nothing of what happened?

266

...you discovered that you were switched at birth and went home with the wrong parents?

267

...you could kill someone and get away with it?

268

...you were at a dinner party where the host served a strange dish that didn't look very appealing?

269

...someone you cared for deeply was dying in great pain and asked you to put him or her out of his or her misery?

270

...you could choose how you are going to die?

271

...a friend got you with a terrific practical joke?

272

...you saw a small wounded animal
by the side of the road?

273

...you discovered a good friend
selling hard drugs?

274

...you could design your own funeral service?

275

...you could choose the physical
appearance of your children?

276

...you were at a friend's home for lunch
and found a fly in your soup?

277

...you knew you were going to go blind in
48 hours?

278

...you could change anything about the
way your parents brought you up?

279

...you could change your physical appearance whenever you cared to?

280

...you went to a movie with a friend and, a third of the way into it, you found it offensive?

281

...you could go into the past but not return?

282

...you could go into the future but not return?

283

...you could control and guide your dreams?

284

...you could go back in time and change one decision you made in your life?

285

...you were asked to run for President of the United States?

286

...you couldn't watch television for one year?

287

...you could communicate with animals?

288

...your parents didn't care what grades you received?

289

...you could wear anything you wanted to school?

290

...you could grade your teachers?

291

...you could design your own ultimate birthday party?

292

...you found out your friend was being abused by his or her parents?

293

...you got a gift from someone you really disliked?

294

...you could design your own bedroom with no limit on what you could spend?

295

...you had a magic eraser and could wipe out one part of your life?

296

...you could peek into any place in the world right now?

297

...you could set your own allowance?

298

...you saw your parents cry?

299

...you didn't have to go to school?

300

...you were six inches taller?

301

...you were six inches shorter?

302

...your girlfriend/boyfriend cooked you a meal that you thought was terrible?

303

...you found a pill that would make you feel happy all the time?

304

...you dove into a crowded pool
and your bathing suit came off?

305

...you could shrink every evil person in
the world to a height of two feet?

306

...you had magic dust that could turn
hate into love?

307

...you could release one prisoner from any
prison in any time in history?

308

...you had super hearing?

309

...you were on trial and needed a
character witness?

310

...you legally didn't have to wear
clothes in public?

311

...you got a tattoo?

312

...you had a big fight with your parents over using the telephone?

313

...you looked exactly like a superstar?

314

...you could have any pet in the world?

315

...you shrank to half your size each month, again and again, until you were no bigger than an ant?

316

...you would grow one inch each week forever?

317

...your nose grew longer each time you lied?

318

...you saw a miracle?

319

...you designed the perfect date?

320

…your parents didn't approve of the person you were dating?

321

…you argued with your parents over the condition of your bedroom?

322

…church was boring?

323

…a date wanted to get physical?

324

...you were really depressed and
needed a good time?

325

...you received a "Dear John" letter and
needed a shoulder to cry on?

326

...you needed money but could
not explain why?

327

...you were at a crossroads in your life
and needed some good counsel?

328

...you had to describe your life as
an amusement park ride?

329

...you needed to break up with someone
you had been going with for a year?

330

...your friend of another race was exclud-
ed from a party given by the popular
crowd you wanted to get in with?

331

...you were the friend of a teen who was
just expelled from school?

332

...your parents, who drink alcohol, told you to stay away from drugs?

333

...you had been Peter when he denied Jesus?

334

...you had been one of Jesus' disciples when their boat was about to sink?

335

...you told your family about some struggles you are going through?

336

...you weren't sure this very moment is a dream or reality?

337

...you could ask Jesus one question about your faith?

338

...you had been one of the disciples when Jesus washed their feet?

339

...Jesus were to ask you the same question he asked Peter: "Who do you say that I am?"

340

...you could compare your life to a football game?

341

...you decided to commit your whole life to God?

342

...you had to pick a car that symbolized you in some way?

343

...you had to pick a farm animal that symbolized the way you see yourself?

344

...you had to pick a color that revealed your personality?

345

...you had to pick a slogan that fit your life?

346

...you didn't agree with a friend's behavior?

347

...your best friend wanted to cheat off your test?

348

...you were in trouble and needed someone to talk to at 3:00 a.m.?

349

...you could give three things to a younger family member?

350

...you wanted to deepen your spiritual walk?

351

...you were asked to pull the lever that would electrocute a convicted serial killer?

352

...your school required all students
to wear uniforms?

353

...you were asked to describe heaven?

354

...you could ask God to solve one
problem in the world?

355

...Jesus visited your school today?

356

...you could plan one perfect day?

357

...you could ask one question
about Christianity?

358

...you were asked to describe three secrets
of a lasting friendship?

359

...you could eliminate one food from
the face of the earth?

360

...you were leaving for an uncivilized continent and could only take five things with you?

361

...a non-Christian had three minutes to live and wanted to know how to become a Christian?

362

...you were at a toy store and had $500 to spend?

363

...someone wanted to make a movie about your life and you could choose the actor or actress who would play you?

364

...you had to describe your parents without using words?

365

...you could have talked to Judas a week before Jesus' crucifixion?

366

...you could change one thing about the way your mom and dad talk to each other?

367

...you could interview your favorite music group?

368

...your country were to go to war?

369

...your dad left your mom and moved
in with another woman?

370

...you were elderly and your family
decided to move across the country?

371

...you were not good enough to compete
in any sport?

372

...you went to a party and realized marijuana was being smoked?

373

...you were asked to contribute money to help a friend get an abortion?

374

...you got a huge zit on your nose the day before the homecoming dance?

375

...you could do the seventh grade over again?

376

...you could be someone else?

377

...you could live in any period of history?

378

...your friend's father suddenly died?

379

...your best friend moved away?

380
...you heard your parents argue and fight?

381
...you got a terrible haircut?

382
...you were being pressured to have sex?

383
...your pet died?

384

...you were called on by a teacher in class when you didn't know the answer?

385

...you were at school when you realized you had forgotten your lunch and had no money?

386

...you were going out on your first date?

387

...you lied to your parents and got caught?

388

...you could change one thing in your church's worship service?

389

...your life were boring?

390

...someone disagreed with you?

391

...you felt lonely?

392

...a friend telephoned when you were watching a good television program?

393

...you could pray for only one thing?

394

...you had a friend who lied about you behind your back?

395

...you had a product to sell and wanted to advertise it?

396

...you sat down in the cafeteria at school and two of your friends were making fun of someone at the next table who said grace before eating?

397

...you felt far away from God?

398

...your parents blamed you for their divorce?

399

...everything you typed on your computer came true?

400

...you found a pornographic magazine?

401

...you were asked to list the three
heroes in your life?

402

...you were an unmarried, pregnant
15-year-old?

403

...you saw a bottle of whisky in the
school locker next to yours?

404

...your friend told you crude/gross jokes?

405

...you had a book report due in three days on a book that has been made into a movie?

406

...your best friend was being two-timed by your older brother or sister?

407

...a homeless shelter opened in your neighborhood?

408

A halfway house for paroled prisoners opened in your neighborhood?

409

...you had to decide between two applicants for a public teaching position, with the most qualified applicant an atheist and the second most qualified applicant a Christian?

410

...you adopted a child and five months later the biological parents wanted the baby back?

411

...you were invited by the "in crowd" to go see a movie that your parents didn't want you to see?

412

...you're suspended for the cherry bomb that your friend threw in the school toilet?

413

...you found out that your friend is homosexual?

414

...a month after you wrecked your parents' car, you scraped the side of the repaired car against a fence?

415

...you had been the paralytic whose friends took you up on the roof, removed the tiles, and lowered you into the room where Jesus was teaching?

416

...an angel appeared to you and promised to answer one question about death?

417

...a woman became president of the United States?

418

...Jesus would heal one thing in your life?

419

...you could build your dream house?

420

...you had to decide whether or not to keep a severely retarded 15-year-old family member on life support?

421

...you were a Christian dating a non-Christian?

422

...you could eliminate one kind of animal from the earth?

423

...you prayed repeatedly for the same thing, but God didn't seem to answer?

424

...you could raise one person from the dead?

425

...your divorced mother were dating a loser?

426

...someone asked you what your ministry was?

427

...your non-Christian parents told you to cut out all of your church activities?

428

...you had to spend three days and three nights in the belly of a whale?

429

...your friend stopped coming to church?

430

...you had to design a ride called "Hell" for an amusement park?

431

...someone you didn't want to date threatened to commit suicide if you didn't date him or her?

432

...a member of your family became President of the United States?

433

...your parents didn't like your friends?

434

...you had been in the boat with the disciples when they saw Jesus walking on the water?

435

...your parents started dressing and acting like teenagers?

436

...you could begin one new tradition in your family?

437

...your youth group were full of phonies and hypocrites?

438

...you could take anyone in the world to meet Jesus personally face to face?

439

...you felt like the ugliest person in school?

440

...Jesus said to you, "What do you want me to do for you?"

441

...you had a camera that took instant pictures of events 24 hours into the future?

442

...you could pass three things on to your children?

443

...food had no taste?

444

...you could plan your own wedding?

445

...you lost 25 pounds?

446

...you were an angel?

447

...you could make someone fall in love
with you?

448

...you could see through walls?

449

...you could never die?

450

...you could write a question for the next *What If...?* book?

You can! Send your questions to:

Les Christie
San Jose Christian College
790 S. 12th Street
San Jose, CA 95112
or fax them to 1-408-293-7352

Resources from Youth Specialties

Ideas Library

Ideas Library on CD-ROM 2.0
Administration, Publicity, & Fundraising
Camps, Retreats, Missions, & Service Ideas
Creative Meetings, Bible Lessons, & Worship Ideas
Crowd Breakers & Mixers
Discussion & Lesson Starters
Discussion & Lesson Starters 2
Drama, Skits, & Sketches
Drama, Skits, & Sketches 2
Drama, Skits, & Sketches 3
Games
Games 2
Games 3
Holiday Ideas
Special Events

Bible Curricula

Creative Bible Lessons from the Old Testament
Creative Bible Lessons in 1 & 2 Corinthians
Creative Bible Lessons in Galatians and Philippians
Creative Bible Lessons in John
Creative Bible Lessons in Romans
Creative Bible Lessons on the Life of Christ
Creative Bible Lessons in Psalms
Downloading the Bible Kit
Wild Truth Bible Lessons
Wild Truth Bible Lessons 2
Wild Truth Bible Lessons— Pictures of God
Wild Truth Bible Lessons— Pictures of God 2

Topical Curricula

Creative Junior High Programs from A to Z, Vol. 1 (A-M)
Creative Junior High Programs from A to Z, Vol. 2 (N-Z)
Girls: 10 Gutsy, God-Centered Sessions on Issues That Matter to Girls
Guys: 10 Fearless, Faith-Focused Sessions on Issues That Matter to Guys
Good Sex
Live the Life! Student Evangelism Training Kit
The Next Level Youth Leader's Kit
Roaring Lambs
So What Am I Gonna Do with My Life?
Student Leadership Training Manual
Student Underground
Talking the Walk
What Would Jesus Do?
Youth Leader's Kit
Wild Truth Bible Lessons
Wild Truth Bible Lessons 2
Wild Truth Bible Lessons— Pictures of God

Discussion Starters

Discussion & Lesson Starters (Ideas Library)
Discussion & Lesson Starters 2 (Ideas Library)
EdgeTV
Every Picture Tells a Story
Get 'Em Talking
Keep 'Em Talking!
High School TalkSheets— Updated!
More High School TalkSheets—Updated!
High School TalkSheets from Psalms and Proverbs—Updated!
Junior High-Middle School TalkSheets—Updated!
More Junior High-Middle School TalkSheets— Updated!
Junior High-Middle School TalkSheets from Psalms and Proverbs—Updated!
Small Group Qs
Have You Ever...?
Unfinished Sentences
What If...?
Would You Rather...?

Drama Resources

Drama, Skits, & Sketches (Ideas Library)
Drama, Skits, & Sketches 2 (Ideas Library)
Drama, Skits, & Sketches 3 (Ideas Library)
Dramatic Pauses
Spontaneous Melodramas
Spontaneous Melodramas 2
Super Sketches for Youth Ministry

Game Resources

Games (Ideas Library)
Games 2 (Ideas Library)
Games 3 (Ideas Library)
Junior High Game Nights
More Junior High Game Nights
Play It!
Screen Play CD-ROM

Additional Programming (also see Discussion Starters)

Camps, Retreats, Missions, & Service Ideas (Ideas Library)
Creative Meetings, Bible Lessons, & Worship Ideas (Ideas Library)
Crowd Breakers & Mixers (Ideas Library)
Everyday Object Lessons
Great Fundraising Ideas for Youth Groups
More Great Fundraising Ideas for Youth Groups
Great Retreats for Youth Groups
Great Talk Outlines for Youth Ministry
Holiday Ideas (Ideas Library)
Incredible Questionnaires for Youth Ministry

Resources from Youth Specialties (continued)

Kickstarters
Memory Makers
Special Events (Ideas Library)
Videos That Teach
Videos That Teach 2
Worship Services for Youth Groups

Quick Question Books

Have You Ever...?
Small Group Qs
Unfinished Sentences
What If...?
Would You Rather...?

Videos & Video Curricula

Dynamic Communicators Workshop
EdgeTV
Live the Life! Student Evangelism Training Kit
Make 'Em Laugh!
Purpose-Driven™ Youth Ministry Training Kit
Student Underground
Understanding Your Teenager Video Curriculum
Youth Ministry outside the Lines

Especially for Junior High

Creative Junior High Programs from A to Z, Vol. 1 (A-M)
Creative Junior High Programs from A to Z, Vol. 2 (N-Z)
Junior High Game Nights
More Junior High Game Nights
Junior High-Middle School TalkSheets—Updated!
More Junior High-Middle School TalkSheets—Updated!
Junior High-Middle School TalkSheets from Psalms and Proverbs—Updated!
Wild Truth Journal for Junior Highers
Wild Truth Bible Lessons
Wild Truth Bible Lessons 2
Wild Truth Journal—Pictures of God
Wild Truth Bible Lessons—Pictures of God

Wild Truth Bible Lessons—Pictures of God 2

Student Resources

Downloading the Bible: A Rough Guide to the New Testament
Downloading the Bible: A Rough Guide to the Old Testament
Grow for It! Journal through the Scriptures
So What Am I Gonna Do with My Life?
Spiritual Challenge Journal: The Next Level
Teen Devotional Bible
What (Almost) Nobody Will Tell You about Sex
What Would Jesus Do? Spiritual Challenge Journal

Clip Art

Youth Group Activities (print)
Clip Art Library Version 2.0 (CD-ROM)

Digital Resources

Clip Art Library Version 2.0 (CD-ROM)
Great Talk Outlines for Youth Ministry
Hot Illustrations CD-ROM
Ideas Library on CD-ROM 2.0
Screen Play
Youth Ministry Management Tools

Professional Resources

Administration, Publicity, & Fundraising (Ideas Library)
Dynamic Communicators Workshop
Great Talk Outlines for Youth Ministry
Help! I'm a Junior High Youth Worker!
Help! I'm a Small-Group Leader!
Help! I'm a Sunday School Teacher!
Help! I'm an Urban Youth Worker!

Help! I'm a Volunteer Youth Worker!
Hot Illustrations for Youth Talks
More Hot Illustrations for Youth Talks
Still More Hot Illustrations for Youth Talks
Hot Illustrations for Youth Talks 4
How to Expand Your Youth Ministry
How to Speak to Youth...and Keep Them Awake at the Same Time
Junior High Ministry (Updated & Expanded)
Make 'Em Laugh!
The Ministry of Nurture
Postmodern Youth Ministry
Purpose-Driven™ Youth Ministry
Purpose-Driven™ Youth Ministry Training Kit
So That's Why I Keep Doing This!
Teaching the Bible Creatively
A Youth Ministry Crash Course
Youth Ministry Management Tools
The Youth Worker's Handbook to Family Ministry

Academic Resources

Four Views of Youth Ministry & the Church
Starting Right
Youth Ministry That Transforms